DAY/BREAK

AMY DAVIS

BOOKLOGIX®
Alpharetta, GA

Copyright © 2025 by Amy Davis

All rights reserved. No part of this book may be reproduced or transmitted in any form or by any means, electronic or mechanical, including photocopying, recording, or any information storage and retrieval system, without permission in writing from the author.

ISBN: 978-1-6653-0969-1 - Paperback
eISBN: 978-1-6653-0970-7 - eBook

These ISBNs are the property of BookLogix for the express purpose of sales and distribution of this title. The content of this book is the property of the copyright holder only. BookLogix does not hold any ownership of the content of this book and is not liable in any way for the materials contained within. The views and opinions expressed in this book are the property of the Author/Copyright holder, and do not necessarily reflect those of BookLogix.

Library of Congress Control Number: 2024926172

∞This paper meets the requirements of ANSI/NISO Z39.48-1992 (Permanence of Paper)

0 3 1 2 2 5

DAY/BREAK

*To those of us who have absolutely no idea
what we're doing . . .
May we find solace together.*

---

*Thank you to those who have dealt with me
at my lowest . . .
Thank you to the friends who will hopefully
always meet me where I'm at . . .
Thank you.*

CONTENTS

Preface	*ix*
My First Prayer	1
Kaleidoscope	6
Underwater	7
Dear Past Self	8
Marker Swords	9
Perhaps It's Me	12
"Step One"	13
Sugar	14
Past Lives	15
Emergency	17
Monkey See	18
Goodnight	19
A Lizard's Tail	23
Epitome	24
Mother's Advice	25
Tire Swings and Honey Sandwiches	26
The Speed of Sound	30
Nightmare	31
Kind Offers	32
Wilting Roses	33
Hallow	36
Translucent	37
Old Me	38
Transit	39
"Step Two"	43

Take a Breath	44
Scaling	45
Being There	52
Contemplation	53
My First Prayer [Extended]	54
"Step Three"	58
Coma	59
String Lights	60
"I'm Just Tired"	61
Apnea	64
Pressure	65
Blurry	67
Obituary	68
Too Late	71
Taking a Tumble	72
Bare Minimum	73
"Step Four"	77
Dear Future Self	78
Pedestal	79
Growth	80
Being Selfish	85
Low Percentage	86
Disappearing	87
Platonic Catastrophe	88
Fairytale Ending	89
Spring	95
Eventually	96
Ice	97
Please, Ask Again	99
"Step Five"	100
Acknowledgments	*101*

PREFACE

Hello, welcome—

It's a pleasure to have you here.

May I please preface with . . . this poetry collection holds both hope and desperation. Within these pages, there's an intentional sense of whiplash between topics due to the struggles I face daily. The highs and the lows, rational against irrational, joy yet . . . depression.

In turn, I wanted to represent myself as an author and individual by sharing with the readers the "good" versus "evil" fight which encompasses myself constantly.

Also, the "light" which clears my mind is the presence of the Lord. I have recently rediscovered my Christian faith; therefore, much of this collection will reference Him. Despite this fact, there's still an awareness of mental health and the illness thereof.

To those of us who both claim the faith and face mental instability . . . It's okay. The goal has always been progress—no one is perfect.

AMY DAVIS

We all must face our demons, whether religious or not.

My wish [and prayer] is that we all might make it through this living Hell we call "life." May we do it, hand in hand . . .

Together.

MY FIRST PRAYER

I see them in everything,

In the way stop lights flash
Green
To yellow
To red—

In the way trees wave as they breathe.

As I drive by,
The music blaring from my speakers,
It leaves me somehow
Both whole *and* empty at the
Same time.

I am a can waiting to be consumed,
My entire purpose
Wrapped within the idea that I exist to
Nourish others.
To nurture the figures whom invade
My memories similar to a pet
You're not quite ready to let go of.

I see them as miracles,
As if they

Are the very air in which I
Inhale.

They are the beauty of a new day,
A fresh start,
Both the sunrise *and* sunset,
Showing me what
Mercy
Looks like.

Above all
I see them in
God's grace . . .

Lord, do I see them within God's grace.

His radiance reminds me that
We are strong,
That we will make it through this,
That our arguments
Will eventually pull us
Closer,
Because it is His will.

What is meant to happen
Will happen.

I remember the before,
The during . . .
The after.

MY FIRST PRAYER

My mind swallows me—
Plays our memories upon the
Back of my eyelids,
Showing me all the good times we had.

Their figures appear within
Shadows *and* sunlight.

The clouds shape themselves into
Butterflies
And
New quest lines from a
Video game
I didn't know I was
Playing . . .

Because I see them.
The friends I once had,
The people I miss,
Wanting so *badly* to
Start over.
To learn each other again,
To discover the *new* "us"—
"Us" being the family
We can grow into
Now that we know what we're
Capable of.

And I see them . . .

AMY DAVIS

Despite having been so
Badly blinded
Before.
I can imagine the way their irises
Flicker
Brown and blue
With every blink—
As if God had brought the
Earth and Sky
In for a kiss
After decades of being in the
Dark.

Each bird which flutters by
Leads my gaze in *their* direction,
Those tired wings gliding
So swiftly
Upon our World's labored breathing—
The wind;
A sweet smell permeates the
Air thereafter,
[A residual effect of an angel's presence,]
And I pray *that* scent might
Stay just a moment longer . . .

I can only hope that
One day
We can return *home* to
One another.

MY FIRST PRAYER

In my pleas to the Lord,
I beg for our bonds
To be reforged stronger than
Before.
And
Now,
Having grown into ourselves
In the *absence* of one another,
I ask Him to allow us the
Capacity for everything which
Might come our way.

May we be able to
Love
So much m*ore*
Than originally expected,
Because
There only exists two necessities
That make life worth
Living anymore . . .

God

And
Each other.

KALEIDOSCOPE

I'm waiting patiently for the person who
Sees my shattered heart,
Picks up every last piece,
Their hands bleeding,
And helps me glue
Myself back together into
A masterpiece.

UNDERWATER

I like being able to
Breathe.

Too bad
Recently
I've come down with
Bronchitis
And the
Inability
To care.

It's so hard
To keep
Going when you're
So used to
Holding your
Breath.

DEAR PAST SELF

Please don't cry.
You're doing just fine.
You'll make it through,
Despite the rain . . .
You'll make it
Home
Eventually.

MARKER SWORDS

When I was a kid,
I used to make swords out of markers,
Swinging with all my might just to watch
their bonds
B   R   E   A   K
Whenever they hit something.
The markers would shatter all OveR the floor,
[Secretly melting through the wood and carpet]
On a journey
D
O
W
N
Into the center of the ea[markers]rth.

I'd line chairs in
two by
two rows
(a larger chair set in front of the other four),
Pretending I was on a bUmPy road
Headed to the
    cOre
of our planet,

AMY DAVIS

Falling   O
                           V
                                  E
                                        R

When the heat melted the ship,
Surfing on the lava ^^^ UP
towards the ocean where I would face
    The **Kraken**!
Grabbing my iron sword and
THRUSTING
with all the strength I could muster.
Just to be JOLTED . . .
Back to reality . . .
to find more markers
bro   /   ken
    On the floor . . .

Wow! What an adventure!
The aftermath a room with a floor made of solid
mess ranging from
StuFFed animals
To stray coloring pages with ScribbleS SS S SS SS S
depicting monsters I always defeated!
A new day meant a *NEW* monster to beat!

But . . . little did I realize that later in life I wouldn't
have to create my own monsters,
One eyEd, green skinned, rotten teethed,
Abominations,
Some I can't conquer like I used to . . .

MARKER SWORDS

Thus
making my successes mean
    MORE!
That training would show me how to use my hands,
Punching
and
kicking
The most vulnerable places,
Grabbing for skin but only finding!?!?
                                        ~ ~ ~ glass . . .

And then watching my palms bleed . . .

BUT *I* was raised in a generation taught to fight for what they believe in!

No matter the blood that was shed!

We'd use words
and signs
and strikes
and a
THOUSAND
more ways to fight!

And *YES*—

Including marker swords.

PERHAPS IT'S ME

I wonder if I'm
Lonely,
Because the one person
Who's always with me . . .
Isn't as developed
Or interesting
As they should be.

Myself.

"STEP ONE"

I brushed my
Teeth
Today.

SUGAR

I am convinced that
Clouds
Are made of
Cotton candy,
Because the pinks
And purples
And blues
Of their edges
Look too sweet
To just be
Made of
Water vapor
And
Hope.

PAST LIVES

Nothing
Is the same as it
Used to be.

The air feels different—
How the molecules
Avoid me
Rather than warming my
Chest with their
Hopeful aspirations.

Car rides and
Spontaneous dancing,
Sugary sweets and the
Presence of tequila,
Milk chocolate and
Energy drinks . . .
Even the slightest
Whiff of your perfume
Jolts me into
Our memories—
Switches me from reality into a
Sense of yearning
For a past we've
Long
Forgotten.

AMY DAVIS

We were so happy
Just being
Friends.

And nothing I can do
Will reverse
Our actions . . .
Those hopeless,
Thereafter
Echoes into revulsion.

Time does not
Play into my hand,
Despite my begging and
Bribes.

Instead,
I must live with my
Consequences.

Perhaps—
Eventually—
You'll be able to
Look at me again . . .

Nothing is the same as it used to be . . .

And I'm so . . .
Sorry.

EMERGENCY

Paramedics would make
Great
Race car drivers.

MONKEY SEE

I thought being able
To see
Far Away
Was a superpower.

Turns out,
It's called being
"Farsighted."

GOODNIGHT

I am lost.
My house is
Not a home.
The empty halls—
Walls and doors and floors
Of my newest venture
Have transformed into a
Hollowed
Out *expectation*,
An explanation stemming from
The idea of "maturity,"
Of gaining time,
Of reaching the
Stage in our age
In which we are told
To just "Let go."

"Growth,"
They call it,
When their baby bird
Flutters,
Sputters,
Shutters,
From the nest to
Begin their life
Alone.

AMY DAVIS

Wings glued to their
Sides as they
Fall.
Calling out to their
Mother,
Brother,
Really *any other* who
May be willing to help.
Until,
They are forced to choose,
To spread their wings
Or succumb to the cold,
Hard earth below.

Originally,
I'd wanted this.
An extension of
Freedom
Appealing to the soul
Who craves it.
Yet now . . .
I miss the faces and places
And spaces my family
Once occupied.
But they are *not* one room
Away anymore,
Nor are they coming back
After an errand expedition.
They are too far to
Reach
Upon a moments

GOODNIGHT

Whim.
They remain.
As I have lost
Myself
To the idea of
Elsewhere.

When I moved out
My mother
Stopped
Texting me
"Goodnight."
And
"I love you."
Instead,
Silence and
Anticipation
And the hope thereof
Filled the potential
Of what could've been . . .
What should've been . . .
What used to be . . .

Everything
Changed.

It hurt
Knowing that after
Eighteen years of
Being their blood and
Bones

AMY DAVIS

And the
Spitting
Image of who they
Taught you to be
That you are just a
Fleeting
Thought
In the
Back of their mind
As their days return to
What they once were . . .

Before
You.

A LIZARD'S TAIL

Sometimes

I wish my limbs were
Like my hair
In the hopes that
I might be able to
Cut off
And
Regrow a piece of me
That *they*

Haven't
Touched.

EPITOME

I went from feeling

Nothing

To feeling
Everything

All at once,

And I lost all sense
Of who I was

Before

And who I now am

After.

MOTHER'S ADVICE

Tell everyone else to "fuck off,"

Because one day

The right person will stay

Despite the barbed wire

And broken glass.

TIRE SWINGS AND HONEY SANDWICHES

Do you remember that night—
When the summer came to an end?
As the sun set swiftly beyond the edge
Of the universe
And came back colder the next day?
The winds blew brisk as the moon
Swallowed us with a starry kiss
And the autumn afternoon arrived
Quicker than expected . . .

Do you remember that night—
When the tire swing broke from worn use?
As we replaced the rubber rim with a
Plastic storage bin
And twisted the rope into a knot?
The world swirled and swung and swished
Right by while making us dizzy from our head
To our knees . . .
And we fell—
We forgot the pains from the past, present,
Future.
As if that moment had satiated our agony
With a blurry laugh and a stumbled walk.
We were children taught to respect our elders,

TIRE SWINGS AND HONEY SANDWICHES

To sit on our hands,
And told to enjoy childhood while it lasted . . .
Because those fleeting minutes didn't last forever.

Do you remember that night—
When we snuck out of bed to carve ourselves
A peanut butter and honey sandwich?
Spread the liquids with a knife,
Making more than one,
Than two,
Than three—
Stealing a bite or two in-between.
As the owls and barren branches of the autumn
Trees knocked upon our windows.
We paused and trembled and quaked in remission,
Stood there with our imaginations running
Wild—
Running free—
As we stilled, feet glued to the ground,
Our mind running laps to create images of monsters
Upon the back of our eyelids.
Nightmares shaped their way from the kitchen to
our
Bedroom doorway—
And we stared at the ceiling until the dawn graced
Us with her presence the next morning.

Do you remember that night—
When Autumn became Winter?
Became Spring?

AMY DAVIS

Became Summer?
Became Fall again?
Fall because Autumn didn't sound quite right.
Became Fall
Became falling
Became flooring
Became fresh wounds and furled flags of surrender...
Became a fruitless fight for frivolity.
Oh, where the Fall fell.
Oh, where we fell during Fall...

Do you remember that night—
When this was all merely a dream?
Where the memories faded into a
Conglomeration of emotions that all
Melded to form a moment paused in time?
We forgot the happy, the sad—
The soft and hard—
The sweet and sour—
Thoughts tousling about our brain as we
Focus on the future...
Forgetting the good times and the bad—
Instead, losing the moments we once had
And held within our arms similar to how one holds
a
Child.
Caring for them.
Nurturing them.

TIRE SWINGS AND HONEY SANDWICHES

Until one day . . .
They must ask themselves:

"Do I *really* remember that night?"

THE SPEED OF SOUND

I can no longer listen to my
Old playlists
Without
Thinking of
Them.

NIGHTMARE

I write,
Because
Reality
Doesn't allow me to
Dream.

KIND OFFERS

Don't threaten me with a
Good time . . .

I wouldn't know how to take it.

WILTING ROSES

Roses are like rusted locks.
Hear me out . . . *hands up*
Roses are given as a gift to those we love,
A statement,
That statement is like a promise,
A promise can't be broken
(Not that easily at least) *funny*
And locks can't be broken unless given a key or combination . . .
Or someone snaps the metal with bolt cutters
Anyway *shakes head* a promise CAN be shattered with words or actions,
So, in turn, roses are like broken promises,
Wait, what was I saying?
Doesn't matter because
Roses wilt, and so do dandelions, and every other flower
In fact, I wonder if there's a type of flower named "Dreams" . . .
Probably not
laughs Look at me! I'm rambling!
But I just love roses!
Roses are like courtesy calls,
Figurative kisses,
Both so subtle and sweet
(Unless they're not . . .)

AMY DAVIS

But roses . . .
Roses are like broken teeth and bruises,
They're given to those we SAY we love,
Sometimes during or after fights depending on who we are.
Roses are a let's-make-up flower—
A flower that mends scars,
But never fully . . .
A flower that doesn't stay forever
Like so many partners out there,
Wilting.
Roses
A take-me-back flower,
Second chance flower,
Pull-me-closer and kiss-me-harder flower,
A don't-touch-me-there flower,
Please-stop-I've-changed-my-mind flower,
A throws-a-lamp-against-the-wall flower,
Rose, roses . . .
Roses are like rusted locks . . .
Compromised and weakened by time as they begin to die.
So I guess you could say . . .
Roses are like hours of tears and memories of shouting,
They're an out-all-night-bad-decision flower,
A forgive-me-that-wasn't-really-me-last-night flower,
The run-out-of-words-first-choice-at-florist flower.
Roses are the most hurtful flower,

WILTING ROSES

The he-doesn't-even-know-my-favorite-
flower flower,
And each time roses are placed in our hands
all we can remember are those times,
Roses are an abusive flower,
But we just have to love 'em!
They're beautiful and a
Hey-I-was-thinking-of-you flower . . .
A valentine-proposal flower,
The flower associated most with love,
But did anyone stop to think they became so
popular because
Roses are the cover-up flower,
A please-stop-crying flower,
The I-love-you flower . . .
And that might've been true once
Because you didn't use to be this way . . .
But love between us will always fade in this
toxic relationship.
It's inevitable.
Just like how every rose you ever got me
always wilted.
So now you understand why I can't accept
anymore roses.
Because roses,
Roses are like gates and doors that're
chained shut
With steel links and rusted locks.

HALLOW

I forget to eat so often,
Because I'm used to feeling
Empty.

I've forgotten what it
Feels like to be
Whole
Again.

TRANSLUCENT

It feels like
God
Visits me more
Now
Than when I
Needed him
Most.

But perhaps he's just
Clearer to see
When I'm not
Looking through
Tears?

OLD ME

Sometimes
I ask myself

"What would she think of me now?"

TRANSIT

I'm tired.
Not the type of tired that sleep can fix,
Nor the type in which dreams
Seclude our main protagonist with
Promises and hopes of a future.
No.
Neither is it the type of exhaustion
To which your bed comforts you,
Treats you similar to a child being
Cradled,
And coddled,
And caressed,
Akin to an orphan being accepted into
A new family . . .

Rather,
I'm the type of tired that makes movement
Nearly
Impossible,
The bed opting instead to hold me
Hostage,
Each sheet and soft blanket swallowing
Me whole . . .
It's the type of tired in which day and night
Switch their schedule
To allow my body a feeling of

AMY DAVIS

Safety
Within the light,
When the darkness of midnight teases
Me with nightmares
And unwanted thoughts
And moments of hesitation
And dry tears
Because no matter
How much I feel, the pain
Doesn't ever want to grace my skin through
Tears—
As if the numbness I feel,
The memories that often fade,
And any and all types of alcohol
Don't allow my body to actually feel something . . .
Anything.
I crave the idea of *feeling* again.

I can't help but allow my mind to travel
Freely
Upon the star-lit sky,
To compose riddles and sullen stories
In which veins are nothing more than
Highways transporting their cargo
Using millions of miniature eighteen-wheelers
Just trying not to crash . . .
Or get sidetracked . . .
Or lose their cargo due to bad weather,
Stolen from their source in transit.
It's as if the tearing of my epidermis
Were a broken stoplight,

TRANSIT

A flush of anger and desperation,
The red heat bubbling to the top,
Flooding into a fresh wound no one
Cares to see,
And the insurance companies
Would rather you risk your own life
To ensure their products make the trip
Safely.
But they don't seem to understand the risks,
To weigh each option before the valleys
Begin to grow.
It'll take a miracle for those stocks to
Make their journey throughout my body,
My very soul begging for them to
Cease.

The pump and bump and hum of my
Heart
Paces the trucks,
Sets a speed limit that
I didn't agree to.
My very essence would rather chew
And gnaw
And spit
At the drivers as they guide the cargo into
The array of shipping docks.

Somehow, though,
Despite the rain,
The supplies have made it.
My drivers are experienced at

AMY DAVIS

Dodging potholes and road barricades,
At seeing the traffic before it starts,
Using side roads and taking their loads
Upon lesser-known trails,
And ensuring the job is done right.
They take after me in that sense
Because, against all odds,
I still remain.
A classic women with blood and bones
And tones of blushed cheeks
Brought to color by the fluid getting
Well traveled within my veins . . .

So, yes,
Regardless of the risks,
In spite of the restless bouts of
Tiredness which plagues my daily routine,
I've laid my head to rest again
All the while
My drivers
Continue on their way to and fro . . .
And you'll be happy to know that
They've finally made it home.

"STEP TWO"

I
Ate
Breakfast
For the
First time
In
Weeks.

TAKE A BREATH

Do me a favor
And take a breath—
Not a shallow sputter,
Shutter,
Stuttering
Gulp of air . . .
But a deep inhale
As if the oxygen within
Your grasp might
Disappear
In the moment
Thereafter.

Hold it.

Feel it.

Remember it.

Now it let go . . .

I'm proud of you.
I'm proud that you're here.
So, please,

Remember to *take a breath*.

SCALING

He sits on my right shoulder and
Weeps.
This being which only *I* can see,
He burdens my empty
Personal space,
Makes the space his own,
Moves in furniture like TVs,
And kitchen chairs,
Stacks of dishes,
An ottoman his mother gave him,
And — most importantly —
A bed.

He spruces up the walls of his
Imaginary apartment,
Cooks dinner using a low-watt microwave . . .
Uses a bowl despite needing a
Plate,
But he's making it work.
He sits on his couch,
Lifts up his remote to
Doom scroll . . .
But ends up sobbing instead.
His cold food, dirty shirt, musty cushions,
    and bleached carpet —
All stained by his tears —

Lose their importance . . .
No longer able to distract him
From reality.

The little figure paces the room he
Just decorated,
Throws his meal against the wall,
And takes a pillow to hold
As his
Bed comforts him . . .

My shoulder is so tired,
So worn,
So heavy from carrying his
Tiny presence
Day in
And
Day out,
My muscles ache,
My bones and joints lock beneath the weight.
He occupies a space which I wish were
Empty
Again.

I do not remember a
Time when he
Wasn't there.

He weeps, cries, yells, festers, laments,
Throwing his every thought
My way.

SCALING

He is so loud . . .
I'm surprised my ears aren't
Bleeding as we speak . . .
Perhaps they actually are . . .
Perhaps the red flowing within my
Body
Beckons the figure,
Encourages him . . .
Makes him scream all that much more.

I only see him in mirrors or
Reflections,
He points out my flaws,
Causes me to pick and
Peel and
Prod at my own skin,
He grabs my attention by snapping and
Pointing and
Laughing.
His voice mumbles
Yet
Increases in volume as I try to tune him out . . .

"Lost"
"Disgusting"
"Overweight"
"Obsessive"
"Needy"
"Lonely"
"Pale"
"Unattractive"

AMY DAVIS

"Undesirable"
"Desperate" . . .

He takes everything I
Hate about myself
And repeats each word
Repeats
And repeats and repeats and repeats and—
Reminding me of a mantra . . .
His whispers echo upon my ear canals
As if his voice is the
Only sound to ever exist.
He is so self-centered . . .
Yet only shows himself to
Me,
Too shy to appear for others,
Yet confident enough to keep me up at
Night
With endless "what ifs" and
Reminding me of my flaws.

He's a coward.
Fighting with me.
Convincing me that I am worthless . . .
Reminding me how I've always gauged my
Worth based upon what
Other people
Think of me.

SCALING

But that stops
Now.
Because, now, another figure has appeared.

This one,
Bathed in light,
Lessens my load.
He takes residence upon my other shoulder,
The left,
And lifts my spirits.

I question if this being might actually be

God

Who shares with me my better qualities.

He doesn't use words
So much as he
Takes my hand,
Guides me to the mirror from before,
And sits in front of it,
Cross-legged,
Arms folded,
His eyes meeting mine,
And waits.
Expectant.

Face to face,
He patiently sits as I

AMY DAVIS

Begin to think.
He helps turn my hates into
Healing,
Each insult pulses and
Pulsates into
Positive reinforcement.

"Independent"
"Confident"
"Kind"
"Strong"
"Willing"
"Intelligent"
"Beautiful"
"Home" . . .

But the "home" I'm still working on . . .
In fact,
I'm still working on them all—
Likely always will.

But
At least he's there,
The one I imagine to be the Lord,
Leading me
Yet *leaving* me
Alone
Sometimes
In an attempt to
Teach me
My own self-worth,

SCALING

Because I am worth so much more—
I *deserve* so much more . . .

I may never be someone's
First thought
Other than my own,
But that's fine.

Because
At least I have myself
And the little figures whom remind me
Daily
That I . . .

Am alive.

BEING THERE

Thank you
For
Being there.

You don't know
How much that
Actually
Meant
To me.

CONTEMPLATION

When I have conversations with
God,
He just sits there,
Listens,
And makes me think through
Every option
Without even needing to say
A word.

MY FIRST PRAYER [EXTENDED]

Within them,
I can see it.

Within their eyes,
The radiant coffees and golds of hers,
And the crystal ocean hues of his,
I can see what
Peace
Looks like.

I can see life,
It's bright longevity,
And within them
I can picture myself
Alive.

For once,
I've seen how beautiful
God
Created us to be —
How we each fill something
In one another that
The others lack,
Us always teaching and
Learning and
Discovering

MY FIRST PRAYER [EXTENDED]

New ideas.
Together.

I'd be lying if I
Refused
To admit
I loved them,
Because
I do.
My adoration for them often
Shapes itself into a
Balloon which hovers just
Out of reach,
Unable to pop—
A symbol of
Public endearment which calls the
Sky above
Home.

Similarly,
They are my *home.*

I find them as my
Shelter
When the weather outside
Runs cold
Or as my
Protection
When the clothes upon my back
Succumb to harsh elements.

AMY DAVIS

Their embraces equate to the entirety of
Spring . . .
So fruitful,
So prosperous.

They are the pieces of myself
I didn't know were
Missing . . .
And that I so desperately
Needed.

Without them,
Who knows where I'd be now?
Who would *they* be?
Who would *I* be?

For once,
I feel as if I am valuable.
It's as if my time on Earth has not been the
Waste
I thought it was.
No,
They are a sign from
God
That he has a plan.

This is the great Lord's creation!
And my! Isn't it beautiful?
Aren't *they* beautiful?

I am beautiful.

MY FIRST PRAYER [EXTENDED]

And it only took this moment,
A fleeting minute while on vacation,
To fully realize it.

God is good,

All the time.

And all the time . . .

God is good.*

*[last four lines of poem]
Illusion to how many Christian denominations close their services.

"STEP THREE"

I made my
Bed,
Washed laundry,
And unloaded the
Dish Washer.

COMA

Being a child and
Needing God is like
Using a tourniquet for a
Scraped knee.

But needing the Lord
Now
Is like begging for a band-aid
When you really need
A lung transplant.

I just recently found
God
And it feels as if the
Doctor's finally
Know what they're doing.

STRING LIGHTS

We don't use
The big,
Overhead
Light
In my house,
Because it
Reveals too much
About my situation.

I'd much rather
Stay in the dark.

"I'M JUST TIRED"

I don't think you understand . . .
When most people say they are tired
They mean to say
That they woke up early
After a late night out,
And just needed another
Hour
To keep the bags from
Appearing beneath their
Eyes.

But when I say I'm tired
I actually mean to say
I have no energy.
I mean
That I didn't sleep last night,
Because the world is
So quiet in the dark
And my thoughts
Are so loud . . .
They're like the roommate you never
Asked for but
Have anyway,
Need anyway . . .

Or when I tell you I'm tired

AMY DAVIS

I mean that
No matter the
Amount of sleep which steals my
Days and nights . . .
I can't seem to feel rested,
That my lack of energy has me tied
To my bed and my eyelids
Sewn shut.

When I say I'm tired
I mean I'm having
A bad day
I mean I haven't eaten since last night,
I *mean* I haven't taken out my trash,
Washed my dishes,
Done my laundry,
Checked my mail,
Taken a shower in days,
Felt like myself.
The old self.
The *happy* self.
The self I hope to return
To one day.
The self who I hope will
Visit every
So often,
The self who held my hand and
Told me I was doing a great job.
I hope she knocks on my door *one day*
To surprise me with flowers and
A new haircut.

"I'M JUST TIRED"

She is the one to show
Me that
Despite her trauma,
She still believes that there is good in
Everyone.
She sees the glass half full when
It's so close to being empty—
There's one droplet
Left upon
The rim with plans to evaporate in
Three seconds.
I want to see her,
Tell her to come in,
And show her what she's become.
I want her to tell me I'm doing great,
Because I've done my best.

My "I'm tired" is a deflection
A distraction
A lie
To avoid any and all types
Of conversation.

But for right now . . .
Since you asked earlier,

"Me? I'm fine. I'm just tired today."

APNEA

I don't
Mind
Snoring,
Since it helps me
Answer
The question:
"If a person snores in their sleep
And no one's around to hear it,
Did they actually make a sound?"

PRESSURE

I just want to be held,
To feel the touch and
Love and pressure
Of someone else there
Beside me . . .

I use one side of the bed
For the potential—
For the *idea* of whom
Might one day fit there.

They say humans need love,
Affection,
They need company,
They need three hugs a day
Just to survive.

So what does it say that I'm
Still here?

Never having been held
So lovingly,
So tenderly,

AMY DAVIS

With the intention
Of making life worth living . . .

Alone.

BLURRY

One of my eyes
Works better than the
Other,
Because
The other
Prefers
To use its
Imagination.

OBITUARY

"She liked red roses,"
They'll say—
"She found joy in the simplest things,
From watching the sun set and
Listening to the summer crickets chirp
To breathing in the chill of autumn—
She enjoyed being alive."

"She liked games,"
They'll reminisce—
"Every chance she got,
There were cards stacked upon the table surface
Or cardstock boards placed lovingly
Between herself and another—
She enjoyed laughter."

"She liked people,"
They'll express—
"She existed to smile,
To help others and sit with them,
To pat their backs on hard days
And to bore the weight they sported
As a way to lighten their lives—
She enjoyed helping."

"She liked midnight,"

OBITUARY

They'll divulge—
"The darkness wrought inspiration,
Caught her within this looping bout of
Relief as the silence built within her,
Her thoughts echoing about her cranium—
She enjoyed expression."

"She liked spaghetti and tall trees,
Cardinals and sour candies,
Poetry, rainy days, rainy nights,
And snow—
Lord, she adored the snow—
And she liked to read
To sit in front of lit fireplaces,
To cover herself in soft blankets
And to watch musicals—
And she liked daydreaming,
Picking pumpkins,
And belting songs at the top of her lungs on
Long drives—
God, she enjoyed long car rides and being the
Unofficial DJ with a slightly broken AUX cord . . ."

"She loved her family . . ."
They'll cry—
"She loved to spend time with them,
To exist within the same space
Without even needing to say a word;
She loved to visit them
And then say her goodbyes;
She loved knowing she was human,

AMY DAVIS

Knowing that her heart wasn't made of
A gaping hole and thin air
But rather a sponge soaking in
Every beautiful thing she saw or did—
Because those farewell hugs were
Worth the pain of missing them."

"She loved everything.
But above all else . . ."

"She loved . . . to breathe."

TOO LATE

There is
So much
I wish
I could
Tell you.

Too bad
We've already
Said our
Goodbyes.

TAKING A TUMBLE

I wasn't always
Religious
[Despite thinking
I was].

It just took
Falling and
Failing and
Faltering and
Fatigue to finally
Find—

Him.

BARE MINIMUM

Is it too much to ask for the bare minimum?
To have someone there to hug and to hold
You—
You with your heart of gold
And the tendency to give
Everything
To everyone else;
Never asking for anything in return
Wanting nothing more than someone
To open your door,
Or bring you flowers,
Or make you smile
While the world piles up on your shoulders
Weighing you down as if
You're a corpse held beneath the ocean
Surface with a cinder block . . .
Unable to breathe in the density . . .
Left within the ebbing coastal waves
For all eternity in blissless
Solitude.

Is it so *hard* to ask for someone to love you?
In those lonely moments at the
Stroke of midnight
When the clock echoes a melody of
Chimes within the walls of your empty

AMY DAVIS

Home—
Though *home* might not be the best word
For your situation . . .
More like a broken record whose scratches
Separate into a bottomless canyon,
A sea of desperation pulling at your heart
Until loneliness gives way to
Heartbreak—
If only you had one to break in the first place . . .

Who do you dream of when there's only air?
Your hands grasp for sheets and silk
As your bed cradles you ever so
Gently—
Your room becomes a sanctuary
For all the thoughts and needs you wish
Someone else could fulfill . . .
Thoughts of another's touch
Play in the forefront of your mind
As your hands trace the skin they might find
Empty—
But also soft . . .
A fever of budding heat whispering
Secrets upon your begging surface . . .
Lo, the image of love transforms on the
Back of your eyelids to reveal
A figure whose shape leaves nothing more
To desire . . .

Who will save me from myself?
When the world begins to darken,

BARE MINIMUM

To shatter around me similar to
A church's stained glass and steeple
Still left alone to deal with the winds of time . . .
Who will shield me
From life as the piles upon my back
Continue to grow
And shift their shape
And fester similar to an infected wound —
Me, wound up as if I were a doll whose strings
Were glued to a music box unable to
Produce even a single
Sound . . .

Is it too much to ask for the bare minimum?
To have someone there to hug and to hold
You —
You with your heart of gold
And the tendency to give
Everything
To everyone else;
Never asking for anything in return
Wanting nothing more than someone
To open your door
Or bring you flowers
Or make you smile
While the world piles up on your shoulders
Weighing you down as if
You're a corpse held beneath the ocean
Surface with a cinder block . . .
Unable to breathe in the density . . .
Left within the ebbing coastal waves

AMY DAVIS

For all eternity . . .
In blissless
Solitude.

"STEP FOUR"

I went
Outside
And
Took a
Breath.

DEAR FUTURE SELF

I don't have much to say . . .
Nor much to ask . . .
But would you at least
Be able to tell me
If we're happy?

PEDESTAL

Even though the wild flowers grow
Where the roses are supposed to bloom,
There are those roses who
Defy all odds to exist,
And when they grow,
They grow taller than the mountains;
Viewed as more than just some object
Thrown into the atmosphere;
Bought in bulk during the cusp of winter
As a symbol of adoration . . .
And here we stand,
All of this,
All of *us*,
We are
Those
Roses.

GROWTH

I'm not who I used to be—

Who I *was*
And
Who I *am*
Are ever changing,
Filtering into the
Expectations of
Society as the
Minutes I've spent in
Solitude pulse into
Years.
Seconds into
Days into
Decades,
Hopping along the
Earth's
Rotating
Tectonics as they, too,
Succumb to time . . .

I can only wonder
How long I have
Left—
Will I fade similar to
Copper within the

GROWTH

Elements?
Will my original color
Transpire into a
Film of
Oxidation and
Seafoam
Hues?

Perhaps
I've forgotten my
Purpose?
Did I ever have one?
Did I begin
Life under the
Impression that I'd
Eventually make a
Difference?
Misled, lost . . .
I am but a
Blip upon the
World's radar that will
Eventually return to the
Soil to toil and coil around the
Oil deposits humanity has boiled into
Miles of aluminum foil and
Fuelled turmoil.
I will return
One day to the ground which

AMY DAVIS

Beckons us back with a
Wink and the
Sweet scent of fresh fruit . . . —
We will all return home one day.

However,
Rather than play into the
Hands of Mercy
This soon in my life,
I sit upon the
Precipice of Fate as she
Teaches me new lessons instead.
She teaches me how to dream,
How to overcome old habits,
And how to age with a
Grace many others may lack.
Knowledge, give me it all;
Give to me the
Tools to build myself into a
Being that's as close to
Perfection as human
Nature allows.
Stand before me to
Shape my growth into the
Branches,
Beaches,
Bastions this planet craves . . .
Because I am dough
Kneading to expand.
I am thus proof that we are all

GROWTH

Seeds sown into the
Fabric of the
Universe,
Our souls designing themselves as
Stars and
Constellations which
Pattern our galaxy
Effortlessly.

How beautiful—
Both you and me . . .
We continue to improve
Together as if existence would
Never have come to
Fruition if not for the
Gravity we exert!
Grab my arm and
Mold me into the
Hug we've both been
Begging for upon our
Birth,
Because
Society has taught us
Independence since
Conception.

AMY DAVIS

I am here,
You are here,
We are here—
Together.

So, I posit the statement previous:

I'm not who I used to be—

BEING SELFISH

I have never been the
First
Choice . . .

And that's okay.

I'm my *own*
First
Choice
Now.

If I'm not there for
Myself . . .

Who will be?

LOW PERCENTAGE

Some days are
Better
Than others.

We can't give
100 percent
All the time.

Just do your
Best,
Because that's
All
Anyone
Can ask of
You.

DISAPPEARING

Do they
Think of
Me
As much as I
Think of them?

Do they
See me
In the way
Seasons
Change or
When the
Wind
Smacks
Their cheeks with
Simple kisses?

Or
Am I
An
Afterthought
Now that
We don't
Speak anymore?
I hope they still
Think of me.

PLATONIC CATASTROPHE

I never knew

Broken
Hearts

Weren't exclusive to

Romantic interactions.

FAIRYTALE ENDING

So, you know how every fairytale begins with a
"Once Upon a Time"
And ends with a "Happily Ever After"?
Well, every story I've been through usually
ends with my body tangled in a wall of
barbed wire
And a shove down a cliff.
Every story begins at the bottom and ends with
a body thrown out into the air
Limbs splayed out into the atmosphere grasping
for anything they can
Trying to grow wings so that maybe,
Just maybe,
The story can start with an already positive outlook,
The wings carrying them through each page,
Skipping from the beginning to the end.
Each fairytale character viewing the pages of an
open book with a title polished
And referencing their own name
But why would they want to start from the bottom
of a mountain when they can
Just set one foot ahead of the other on the page where
their "happily ever after" actually comes true?

Sometimes,
I like to dig my eyes into the last page of a story

AMY DAVIS

So that I know what's going to happen.
A story isn't spoiled by a little peek into the future,
But can draw the reader into a frenzy
Gripping them tighter than any first sentence could,
And while knowing the ending can taint the mind of the once eager audience,
It will never NOT have a meaning that's a thousand times deeper
You just have to read the story to find it
Like a word search where that last word is impossible to find
Usually a word that's super simple
But in this arrangement and sea of stray circling lines
You just can't seem to complete the hunt.
There's this thirst, a passion to see where it's hiding,
An overwhelming display of both anger and accomplishment
When you understand what you were doing wrong,
You figured out the meaning of that oh-so simple phrase,
circle the word,
Just as you would feel when staring at the puzzle for long enough
The word hidden in plain sight
A pair of fresh eyes able to spot each letter individually
to make the word connect
"FOUND IT!"

"It" isn't a word but a cure,

FAIRYTALE ENDING

We found "it"
An endless magnitude of fairytale endings that teach us to listen to what we're told,
They teach us about this constant and inevitable danger of the unknown.
Our mothers sit us down to tell us about "stranger Danger" when we should really just open up
A book—
Just look at what happened to Little Red,
The wolf, dressed as her grandmother, a monster hidden in plain sight,
Each question tearing Little Red closer to the fate already set to happen,
No going back.
We, ourselves, never cautious enough,
Drag with us lessons which can be traced back to the repeated actions of the fairytale characters,
Their stories have meanings more than love,
Cinderella and Sleeping Beauty taught us that there are those insolent strangers out there,
Stalkers and figures sneaking into our room at night just
to sneak a peek, gaining the courage to
kiss us after the third night,
Taking our will into their own,
And no matter what we do,
What follows will change the face of our story forever.

AMY DAVIS

Each of us has our own fairytale,
A story we've collected and each memory stowed away
in a single fold of our brain,
Some people give us their happily ever after in documented experiments
Or technological advances,
Maybe one day we can skip the phase in our life where we are pushed into the mud,
Beaten until we're blue,
And we can just meet ourselves in the future as encouragement like
"Keep going, you'll make it.
We can make it."
Maybe if we stood in front of the mirror staring at ourselves in our most honest form,
Facing the reality that our mistakes are what make our stories great
And set a recorder on repeat saying the following looped
phrase in a melodic rhythm,
"You can do it. A new day's ahead."
Then we might be able to stretch our "once upon a time"
into a "happily ever after" (sooner than excepted).
We might be able to grab the first page and the last,
Tearing that ending from the back of the book,
And actually glue it on the second page.

The shortest fairy tale is composed of three words.

FAIRYTALE ENDING

Born and died,
And everything in between a mystery too perfect to
describe.
The "and" is a testimony, a statement, a single reflection
upon life,
It's the longest trail I've ever had to navigate,
And at the end of the trail, there we are standing at the cliffs edge,
Some of us holding hands and others crying because
they regretted not making their story what it could have been,
Sorry, but we can't go back again.
At any moment one of us will be pushed off,
That'll be the end of their fairytale,
And there's always that hope that someone will take
the time to lay down with a cup of hot tea,
Their hands on the photo album in high regards to the memories you made together,
Each picture a chapter,
A welded together string of moments that unfolded to make your life story great
It was a peek into what your happily ever after was always meant to look like.

Each "Once Upon a Time" began long enough ago that
you can understand what I'm saying,

You understand every reference and word falling from
my tongue.
You're already on your way to that "Happily Ever After"
So, don't give into that evil witch trying to kill you faster,
Use your strength to pull you up the steep incline of
the word spelt
N.O.T.H.I.N.G.
Because there will always be something you can do.
Only you can condense the space between "Once Upon
a Time" and "Happily Ever After"
So chop away each letter of the alphabet until the O from
"Once" and the R from "After" can spell the word "OR"
Because there's your perfect story OR there's not.
You make that choice.

Here's my fairytale ending.
I've dragged my story into a single phrase.
"Once upon a time, there was only happily ever after."

SPRING

He sits with me
On my
Front porch
And
We watch
His
Creation
Bloom
After so long of
Being
Dormant.

We're both so
Ready for
New growth.

EVENTUALLY

I am
Deteriorating
Here on
Earth . . .

Because my
Body is getting
Ready for it's
Venture to
The Kingdom of
God.

Heaven.

Here I come.

ICE

I've never felt so helpless!
Movement at this moment
is built upon the theory
that people are meant
to move at all,
Whether forward or
backward or side to
side,
But I . . . can't.
I'm stuck in this eternal
quicksand in which the
sinking sand is frozen
at my waist—
Just enough to prohibit my
leaving and yet still
allowing me to breathe.

Stuck is a light term for my
situation,
More like I'm a brick wall
built thick with each
layer the length of
thirteen human hearts
Stacked and lined up to
take every wrecking ball
hit with grace.

AMY DAVIS

This moment is the
answer to the age-old
question of what would
happen
If an unstoppable force hit
an immovable object.
And I'm not sure I'm ready
to know the answer.

Newton was one hundred percent
correct when he stated,
 "An object at rest will
stay at rest"
But I'm inclined to believe
that "unless acted upon
by an unbalanced force"
is a lie,
Because no matter what
slams into me—
I. Don't. Move.
Tsunamis and tidal waves
are useless acts of
nature that can't take
me anywhere else.
Frozen has never felt so
cold . . .
So . . . difficult . . .

PLEASE, ASK AGAIN

Before you ask,
I'm doing just fine
Today.

I'm going to survive.

My bed will
Let me
Leave in the
Morning.

If you don't
Mind, though . . .
Maybe
Just ask me
How I'm doing
Again
Tomorrow?

Your
Question
Helps me know
Somebody
Cares.
And sometimes . . .
That makes all the difference.

"STEP FIVE"

insert being alive here

ACKNOWLEDGMENTS

I would like to thank everyone involved in the creation of this collection. Editors, planners, designers, and everyone behind the scenes who I may have never met, but still aided the process to create this dream of mine come to fruition. Sincerely, I appreciate your dedication and hard work.

www.ingramcontent.com/pod-product-compliance
Lightning Source LLC
Chambersburg PA
CBHW052148070526
44585CB00017B/2030